AF374806

Australia
ZOO
Home of The
Crocodile Hunter

This book is dedicated to
Adventurers everywhere
Join me in some great adventures

Acknowledgments:
Our Supporters and Encouragers
and to my illustrator T. Vicini

After a wonderful concert, The Wiggles told me I must visit the
Australia Zoo. Which is Steve Irwin's Zoo.
You know, the Crocodile Hunter.

They knew the Irwin Family. They told me how they met and said they would take me for a ride in the Big Red Plane and introduce me.

When we arrived at the Australia Zoo, they introduced me to Terri, Bindi and Robert Irwin. The Irwin's welcomed me and they treated me like an old friend.

Terri took me on a tour around the Zoo and I got
to see a lot of animals native to Australia.

I even saw a giraffe with a neck so long
his head was as high as the sky!

Bindi showed me more of the Zoo. She has an island at the zoo called, "Bindi's Island."

We talked about what it is like to be a Wildlife Warrior. She said that her brother Robert and her mother Terri were both wildlife warriors. I said to myself, "Wow, I didn't know that!

Terri taught me how to feed the kangaroos.
The kangaroos were gentle and sweet.

Next, I held a koala and it was like a dream come true.
The koala was soft and cuddly and it reminded me of a stuffed
animal I used to have when I was young.
You hold it like you would hold a
baby.

I decided to lay against a Eucalyptus tree and watch the kangaroos go by and see the koalas eating the leaves.

I was able to see camels, owls, marsupials, birds, and dingoes in the distance.

Marsupials are mammals who have a pouch on their
stomach to carry their young. Dingoes are native
Australian dogs but they don't bark,
They howl like wolves.

I saw a wombat, numbat, bilby, quoll, and a kookaburra. I even saw a flying sugar glider!

Next it was time to feed the crocodiles... but it was a very long and exciting day and I was getting sleepy.

So I thought I would close my eyes and rest a few minutes.

Then when I opened my eyes, I looked into the sunset and saw the legendary Crocodile Hunter Steve Irwin calling my name!

"G'Day Yahya!"

" You're Steve Irwin aren't you?" Yahya asked, surprisingly shocked. "Yes I am," Steve replied. "Why don't you come on a crocodile hunt with me? "

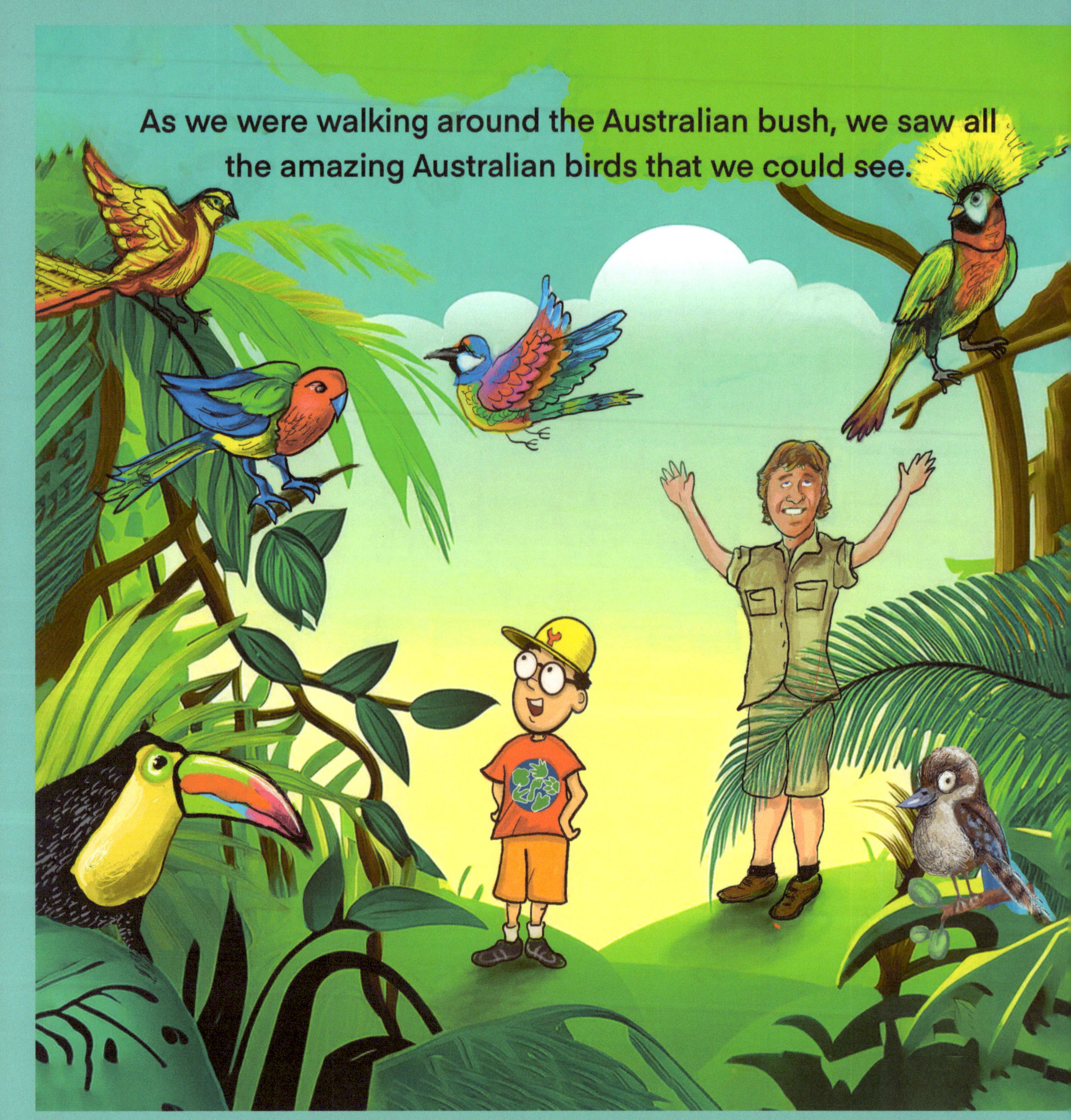
As we were walking around the Australian bush, we saw all
the amazing Australian birds that we could see.

Then he gave me a ride in a boat full of watermelons, and
we started a wild and adventurous crocodile search.

I spotted a massive crocodile over near the shore!

The crocodile was at least 12 feet long! Steve said, "How would you like to feed 'em'? "

Just then, the massive crocodile came up to the boat and Steve handed me a watermelon and he said, "Just drop it in his mouth."

And I bravely put the watermelon in its huge mouth like Steve showed me. Then I helped Steve rescued some baby crocs that drifted too far away from their nest.

We were happy the baby crocodiles were safe, so we headed back to the zoo. Steve thanked me for helping and said I was a true Wildlife Warrior!

When we got back, Steve told me that he had a surprise for me. And told me to close my eyes.

When I opened my eyes I saw the Wiggles, Terri, Bindi and Robert around me. "Why it's a party with all my best friends!"

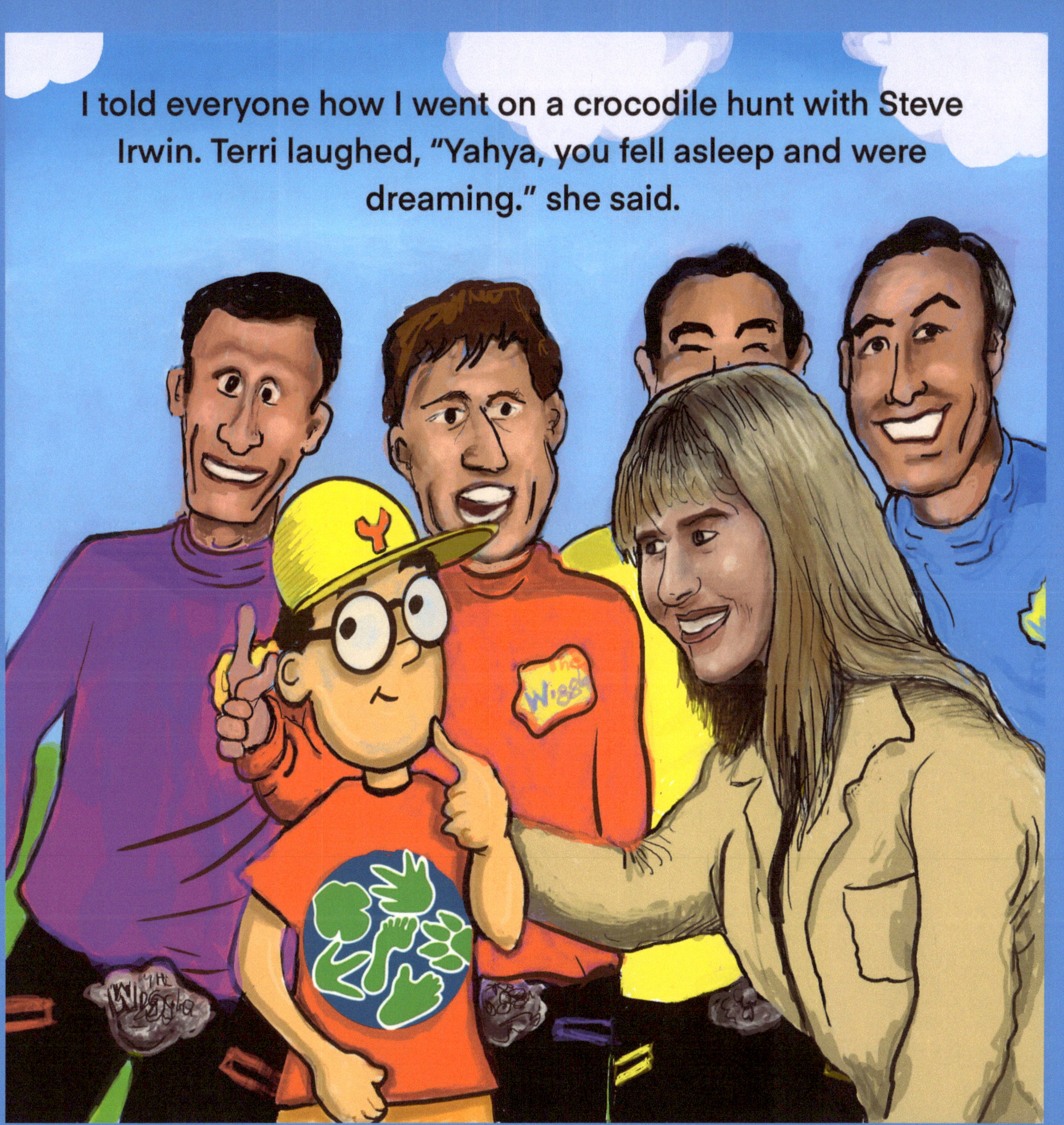
I told everyone how I went on a crocodile hunt with Steve Irwin. Terri laughed, "Yahya, you fell asleep and were dreaming." she said.

"But my dad would have loved that you were a Wildlife Warrior" said Bindi. "Oh, I must have fallen asleep." Yahya said, "But it was the best dream ever!"

As we walked out of the Australia Zoo, I said goodbye to the Wiggles and the Irwin family and promised that we would see them again soon.

Yahya said, "I promise to become the best Wildlife Warrior ever and to help all animals everywhere."
Now on to my next adventure..."

Read the inspiration for this book!

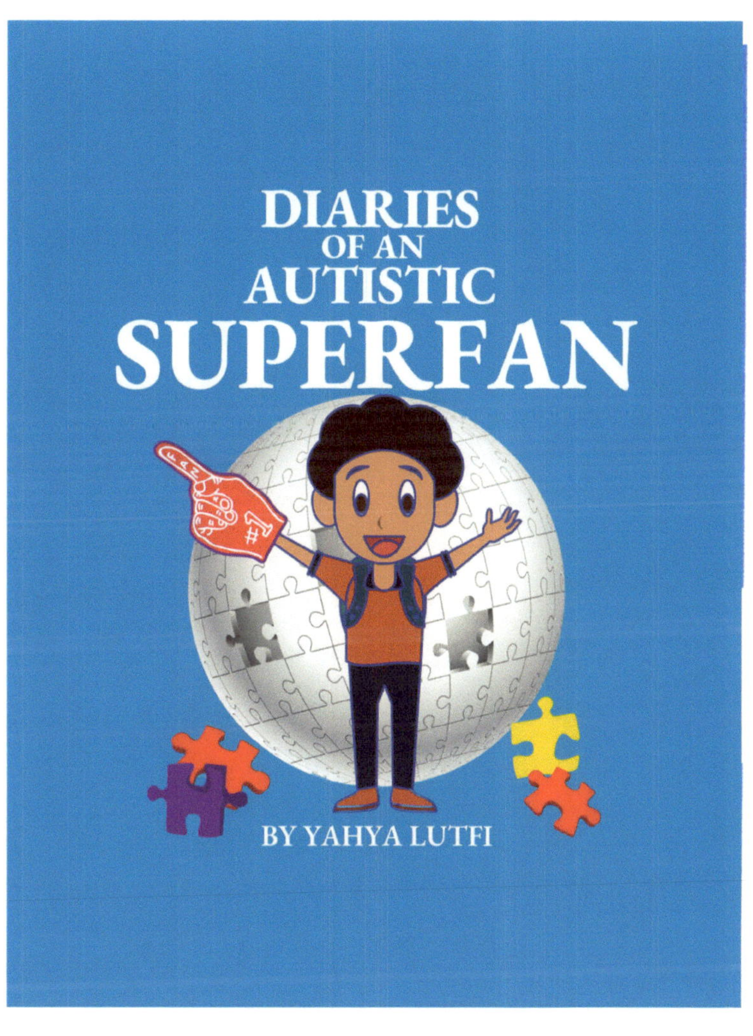

Get the book!